HORSES

THOROUGHBRED HORSES

JANET L. GAMMIE

ABDO & Daughters

Published by Abdo & Daughters, 4940 Viking Drive, Suite 622, Edina, Minnesota 55435.

Library bound edition distributed by Rockbottom Books, Pentagon Tower, P.O. Box 36036, Minneapolis, Minnesota 55435.

Printed in the United States.

Cover Photo credit: Firth Photo Bank
Interior Photo credits: Firth Photo Bank, pages 9, 11
Peter Arnold, Inc. pages 17, 19
Julie Green, pages 5, 7, 13, 15, 21

Edited by Bob Italia

Library of Congress Cataloging-in-Publication Data

Gammie, Janet L.
   Thoroughbred Horses/ Janet L. Gammie.
      p. cm. — (Horses)
Includes bibliographical references (p.23) and index.
   ISBN 1-56239-437-1
1. Thoroughbred horse—Juvenile literature. 2. Race horses Juvenile literature.
[1. Thoroughbred horse. 2. Race horses.] I. Title. II. Series:
Gammie, Janet L. Horses.
SF293.T5G35   1995
636.1'32—dc20   95-1508
                                                        CIP
                                                        AC

ABOUT THE AUTHOR
   Janet Gammie has worked with thoroughbred race horses for over 10 years. She trained and galloped thoroughbred race horses while working on the racetracks and farms in Louisiana and Arkansas. She is a graduate of Louisiana Tech University's Animal Science program with an equine specialty.

Contents

WHERE THOROUGHBREDS
CAME FROM

Horses are mammals just like humans. Mammals are warm-blooded animals with a backbone. Their body heat comes from inside their body.

The earliest **ancestor** of the horse was *Eohippus* (e-oh-HIP-us). It lived about 50 million years ago. There are three different types of horses: hot bloods, cold bloods and warm bloods. These names refer to the horse's birth place and not its body temperature.

Stallions were brought to England from the Orient.

Detail Area

A thoroughbred horse.

Thoroughbreds are hot bloods. Around 300 years ago, three **stallions** were brought to England from the **Orient**. Their names were Darley Arabian, Byerly Turk, and Godolphin Arabian. All thoroughbreds today are related to these three stallions.

The thoroughbred is known for its speed as a racehorse. It is used to create new **breeds** of horses like the **Trakehner** and the **standardbred**.

WHAT THOROUGHBREDS LOOK LIKE

A thoroughbred has large eyes, a well-developed head, a long neck and back, sloping shoulders, a powerful rear end and long legs.

Thoroughbreds come in all shapes and sizes. They weigh 900 to 1,500 pounds (408 to 680 kilograms). The average height is 14 to 17 hands high (hh). Each hand equals 4 inches (10 centimeters). Thoroughbreds can be any solid color.

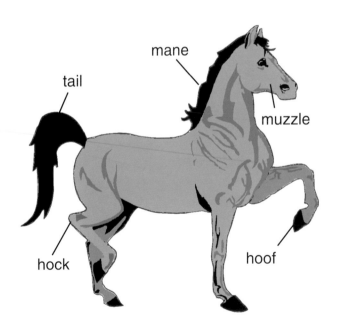

mane

tail

muzzle

hock

hoof

Horses share the same features.

Thoroughbreds have large eyes, a well-developed head, and a long, slender neck.

WHAT MAKES THOROUGHBREDS SPECIAL

The thoroughbred is known for its speed and racing skills. No other breed equals the thoroughbred at racing distances of 3/4 to 1 1/2 miles (1.2 to 2.4 kilometers). The **quarter horse** is also a racehorse but races shorter distances.

Thoroughbreds are not just used as racehorses. They are ridden in **polo**, **steeplechase** racing, and jumping. The most famous race horses are Secretariat and Ruffian. Thoroughbreds are **bred** with other horses to improve the horse's quality. Racing quarter horses are often bred with a thoroughbred to improve their speed.

Thoroughbreds are known for their speed and racing skill.

COLOR

Common colors for thoroughbreds are: bay, chestnut, black, roan, or gray. Bay can be light or dark brown bodies with black points. Roan is one basic color with one or more colors added. Points are the leg, **mane** and tail. A horse with brown hair and the same color or lighter points is a chestnut.

Black horses have all black hairs and can have white markings. Markings are solid white patches of hair found on the head and legs. Gray horses have white and black hairs on black skin. Gray horses often turn white with age.

There are five basic head markings: star, stripe, blaze, snip, and white face. A thoroughbred can have different mixes of these head markings. Leg markings are ankle, sock, and stocking. Any mix of these leg markings are also common.

A thoroughbred with a star head marking.

STAR   **STRIPE**   **SNIP**   **BLAZE**   **WHITE FACE**

CARE

Except for horses that are working, showing, or racing, most horses are happier living on pasture. Horses kept on pasture or in stalls are vaccinated and dewormed often. A vaccination is a shot that protects the horse from disease. Deworming rids the horse of parasites inside the body. Parasites are bugs that live off another animal, causing sickness.

After a horse is two years old the teeth are floated. Floating is filing the teeth so they are even. This allows for proper chewing of food. A horse's **hooves** are trimmed often just like people trim their fingernails. Hoof trimming begins when the horse is about five months old.

Good grooming habits protect the horse from parasites that live on the skin and hair. Grooming is brushing and cleaning the horse's body.

Grooming keeps a horse clean and prevents skin and hoof diseases.

FEEDING

Horses need food to grow and develop. Hay and grain are the two basic types of feed. Hay can be grass or alfalfa. Grains include oats, wheat, barley, and corn. Oats can be mixed with other grains or fed alone. A mix of hays and grains are fed in proper levels to meet a horse's **nutritional** needs.

These needs will depend on age, how well the horse has grown, **training**, and whether or not the horse is **pregnant**. Fresh water should always be given. Horses can live only a few days without water.

Horses need food to grow and develop. Hay and grain are the two basic types of feed.

THINGS THOROUGHBREDS NEED

The saddle protects a horse's back and makes riding easier. There are two basic types of saddles: the Western saddle and the English saddle.

The Western saddle is heavy and bulky. It has long **stirrups**, a large seat, and a horn. It is used for long-distance riding. The English saddle is used for trick riding like jumping. It has shorter stirrups called **irons**. It is lightweight with a smaller seat than the Western saddle.

A thoroughbred racing saddle weighs only a few pounds. The **bridle** goes over

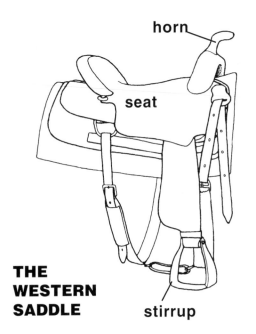

horn

seat

THE WESTERN SADDLE

stirrup

Thoroughbreds use all kinds of equipment.

the horse's head and is used to control the horse. There
is also a **bridle** without a **bit** called a bosal.

HOW THOROUGHBREDS GROW

A baby horse is called a foal. A foal lives inside the mare's body for about 11 months. It takes its first wobbly steps 15 minutes after birth. In about an hour a newborn foal can run.

A foal is born without teeth. It grows a full set of teeth and can eat grass within a week. After 3 to 4 months the foal can live without its mother's milk.

Because thoroughbreds are **bred** to run, they grow fast compared to other breeds. Young horses spend their first year playing and growing. They run, jump and kick just for fun. Playing with other foals keeps the foal strong and healthy. A racehorse is old enough to race in two years and is fully grown in three years.

A foal spends its first year playing and growing.

TRAINING

Training begins early for a racehorse. A few days after birth a halter is put on it for the first time. A halter goes over the horse's head and acts like a collar. As the foal grows it will learn to walk beside a person. As a **yearling**, the racehorse will learn to **lunge** on a lunge line.

A lunge line is a long rope. It is long enough so a horse can walk, **trot**, and **gallop** in a large circle. Walk, trot, and gallop are the three speeds that a horse needs to know.

The horse is saddled when it is two years old. After it has accepted the saddle and rider, the horse will begin its training on the track. A two-year-old thoroughbred can then enter its first race.

Training begins early in a thoroughbred's life. It doesn't wear a saddle until it is two years old.

GLOSSARY

ANCESTOR (AN-ses-tor) - An animal from which other animals are descended.

BIT - The metal piece of a bridle that goes in the horse's mouth.

BREED - To produce young; also, a group of animals that look alike and have the same ancestor.

BRIDLE - The part of the harness that fits over the horse's head (including the bit and reins), used to guide or control the animal.

COAT - A natural, outer covering, such as the hair or fur of an animal.

EQUIPMENT (e-QWIP-ment) - Saddles and bridles.

GALLOP - To run fast.

HOOF - A horse's foot.

IRONS - A type of stirrup.

LUNGE - Any sudden forward movement.

MANE - The long, heavy hair on the back of a horse's neck.

NUTRITION (noo-TRISH-in) - The use of food for energy.

ORIENT (OR-ee-ent) - The countries of Asia, especially the Far East.

POLO - A game played on horseback, using long-handled mallets in an attempt to hit a wooden ball through the opponent's goal.

PREGNANT - With one or more babies growing inside the body.

QUARTER HORSE - A compact muscular saddle horse characterized by great endurance and high speed for short distances.

STALLION (STAL-yen) - A male horse.

STANDARDBRED - A smaller, rugged horse used for harness racing.

STEEPLECHASE - A horse race on a course that has hedges, ditches, and other obstacles over which the horse must jump.

STIRRUP (STIR-up) - Where the feet are placed on a saddle.

TRAINING - To teach.

TRAKEHNER (TRAY-ken-er) - A German horse breed that stems from thoroughbreds and Arabians.

TROT - To run but not fast.

YEARLING - A year-old horse.

BIBLIOGRAPHY

McFarland, Cynthia. *Hoofbeats*: *The Story of a Thoroughbred*. Macmillan Publishing Company, New York, 1993.

Millar, Jane. *Birth of a Foal*. J.B. Lippincott Company, New York, 1993.

Possell, Elsa. *Horses*. Childrens Press, Chicago, 1961.

Index